**Helping Children See Jesus**

ISBN: 978-1-64104-054-9

# Living the Christian Life
### *New Testament Volume 23: Romans Part 5*

Author: Marilyn P. Habecker
Illustrator: Frances H. Hertzler
Colorization courtesy of Good Life Ministries
Typesetting and Layout: Patricia Pope

© 2019 Bible Visuals International
PO Box 153, Akron, PA 17501-0153
Phone: (717) 859-1131
www.biblevisuals.org

All rights reserved. No part of this publication may be reproduced, stored in a retrieval system or transmitted in any form by any means, electronic, mechanical, photocopy, recording or otherwise, without the prior permission of the publisher, except as provided by USA copyright law.

## RELATED ITEMS

To access related items (such as activities, memory verse posters and translated texts) please visit our web store at www.biblevisuals.org and enter 1023 at the top right of the web page. You may need to reduce the zoom setting to get the search box.

## FREE TEXT DOWNLOAD

To obtain a FREE printable copy of the English teaching text (PDF format) under Product Format, please scroll down and select Extra–PDF Teacher Text Download. Then under Language select English before clicking the ADD TO CART button to place in your shopping cart. Other languages are available at an additional cost from the Language menu. When checking out, use coupon code XTACSV17 at check-out and click on Apply Coupon to receive the discount on the English text.

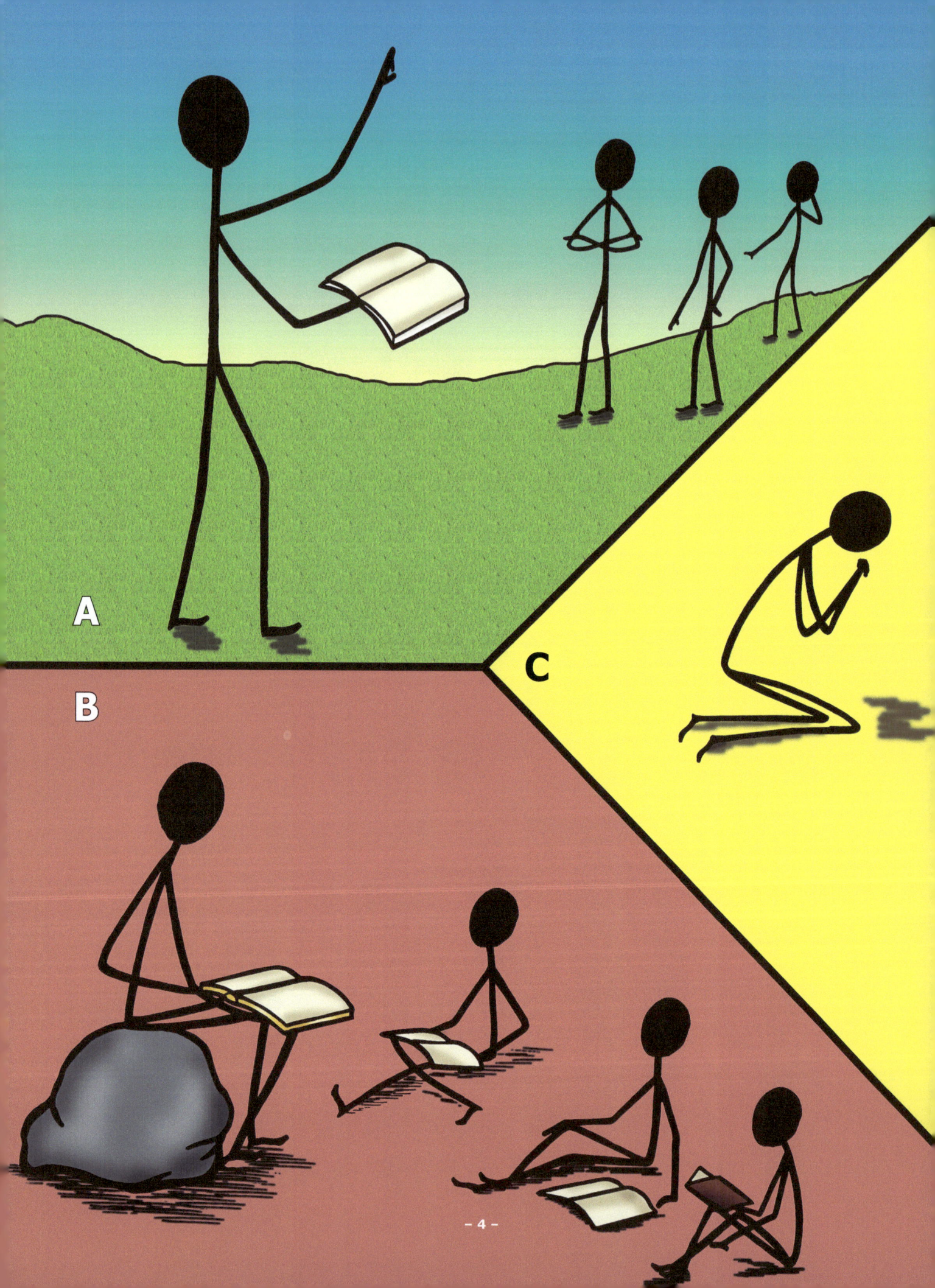

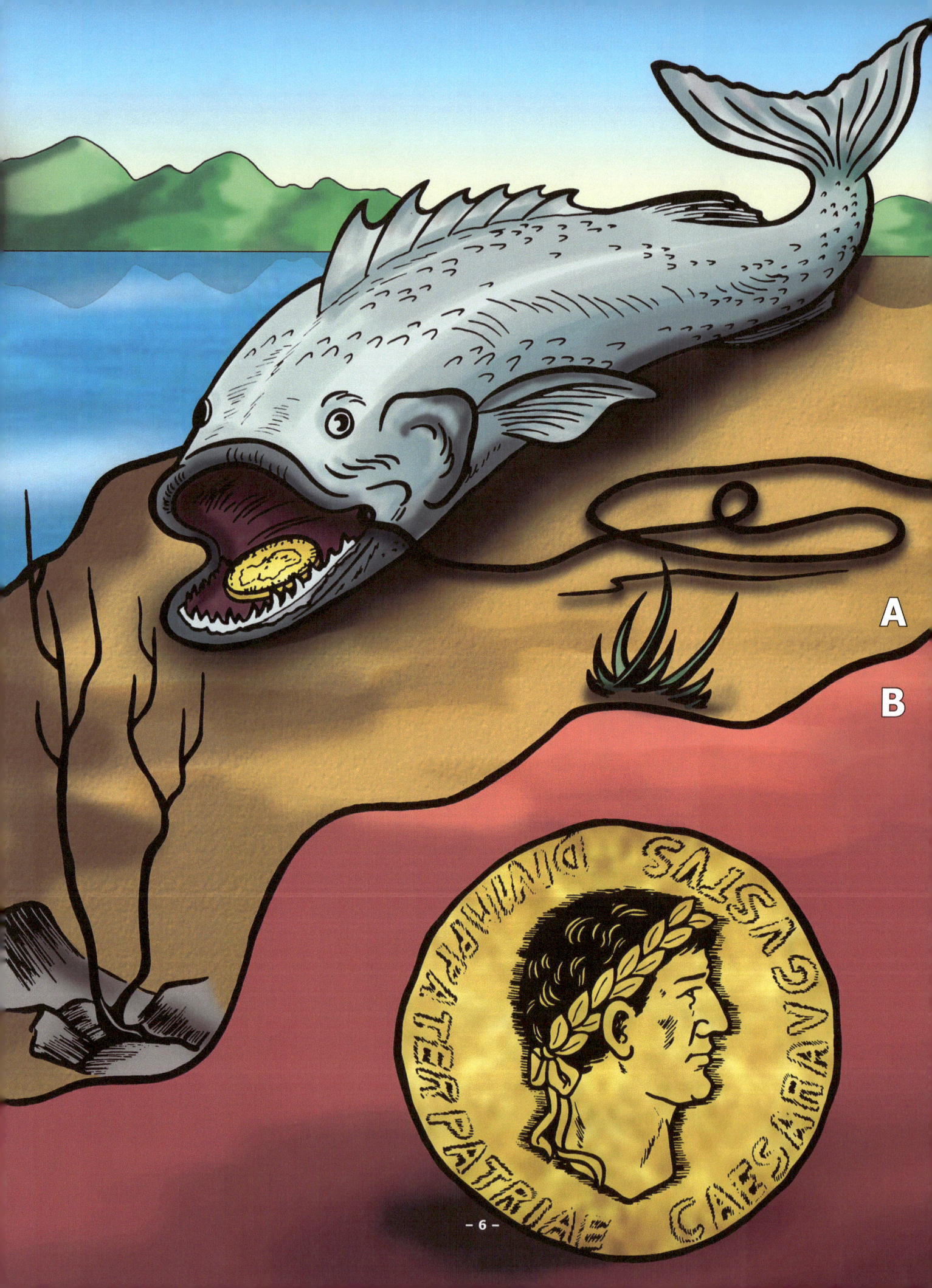

So then every one of us shall give account of himself to God.

Romans 14:12

© Bible Visuals International

# Lesson 1
# CHRISTIAN SACRIFICE

## NOTE TO THE TEACHER

The theme of Romans is the righteousness of God. Paul shows that God is righteous in condemning sinners. He is righteous in sanctifying those who trust in His Son. He is righteous in His dealings with Israel in the past, present and future. In the closing chapters of the book, the Apostle Paul turns to the subject of everyday living. These chapters are extremely practical. From them we learn that God's righteousness produces righteousness in the life of the Christian, enabling him/her to live the Christian life.

Although the lessons in this volume may be easy to understand and perhaps easy to teach, they may also prove to be the most difficult to practice. Pray that the truths contained in these final chapters of Romans may become a vital part of your own Christian experience.

There is an old proverb that says:

I hear . . . I forget.
I see . . . I remember.
I do . . . I understand.

We use visuals like those in this book to help our students remember the lesson. We encourage them to make notebooks so that by writing (and perhaps by drawing simple illustrations), your class members will better retain what has been taught. They will understand the lessons when they practice the things they learn. So we urge you to have class discussions at the end of each lesson, determining particular things which can be done to live out the lesson. Begin lessons 2, 3, and 4 by letting each one tell how he/she practiced the preceding lesson.

**Scripture to be studied:** Romans 12; Genesis 22:1-14; Hebrews 11:17-19

**The *aim* of the lesson:** To teach that God wants Christians to give themselves completely to Him to do whatever He chooses.

**What your students should *know*:** Christians are to be living sacrifices–living lives that please God.

**What your students should *feel*:** A desire to live for God, doing whatever pleases Him.

**What your students should *do*:** Promise God they will do one thing He would have them do this week. Pray, asking God for help to do what they have promised.

**Lesson outline (for the teacher's and students' notebooks):**

1. Abraham receives a love gift from God (Genesis 21:1-8).
2. God asks Abraham for a sacrificial gift (Genesis 22:1-8).
3. God tests Abraham by asking for his son (Genesis 22:9-19).
4. All believers can give themselves to God (Romans 12:1-2).

**The verse to be memorized:**

*So then every one of us shall give account of himself to God.* (Romans 14:12)

## THE LESSON

In his letter to the Romans, the Apostle Paul taught many things. He explained that all have sinned and that God condemns sin. He said that because of God's righteousness He gave His own Son, the Lord Jesus, to die for sinners. Carefully Paul explained that those who believe in Christ are justified–declared righteous by God–the moment they place their trust in Him. Paul continued by showing that all believers in the Lord Jesus are sanctified–set apart by God for His own purpose. Because this is so, Christians are to live pure, separated lives that bring glory, and not shame, to God's name.

Do you remember what it was that filled Paul with sorrow? It was the knowledge that multitudes of Jews had not placed their trust in the Lord Jesus. Many refused to listen to the message of salvation. Therefore they would be forever separated from God. The apostle wrote of God's wonderful plan for the nation Israel: someday many Israelites will claim Christ as Saviour and King, even though they will have to endure much suffering before that time. God, the righteous One, loves the Jews.

Having taught so much, Paul probably asked himself, "What words of instruction shall I send to these Christians? What does God want me to tell them?" Then continuing, he wrote, "Dear Christian brothers, I ask you to give your bodies as living sacrifices to God. He is pleased with this kind of sacrifice."

What did he mean? Are Christians to allow their bodies to be sacrificed in the same way that animals were sacrificed? Oh, no. God doesn't require this. But He does want Christians to give themselves completely to Him, to be used in whatever way He chooses. They are to give up their own plans for their lives. They are to be willing to do whatever God wants them to do. They are to be *living* sacrifices, not dead ones.

Sometimes when we are children, we dream of being older. We try to imagine where we'll live and what we'll be doing. We may plan all sorts of impossible things and hope that they will come true someday. As we grow older, we continue to plan ahead. We decide what we want to do with our lives. We work toward that goal. This is natural. But when we belong to God, we should want to do what He wants us to do with our lives. This is far more important than doing what we want to do. God knows all things. He knows what is best for us. Even though He may ask us to do something difficult, we must trust Him and obey Him. God is pleased when we give our bodies to Him as living sacrifices.

## 1. ABRAHAM RECEIVES A LOVE GIFT FROM GOD
### Genesis 21:1-8

Many hundreds of years before the Apostle Paul lived, God asked Abraham to do something very difficult. Abraham loved God dearly. He had received a special promise from God. God promised to give Abraham and Sarah, his wife, a baby son–though they were much too old to have a baby. Abraham and Sarah believed God, knowing that He could do things which seemed impossible to them. Because they believed God, their faith was rewarded. And one day a son was born to them.

### Show Illustration #1

Abraham and Sarah were happy, so happy that they named their boy Isaac, which means "laughter." Sarah said, "God has made me laugh, and all who hear will laugh with me." They watched their baby grow, thanking God for His wonderful gift. At night, when little Isaac slept, Abraham and Sarah probably talked together of the wonderful promise God had made. He had told them that one day the family of Abraham would number more than the stars in the sky or the sands on the seashore. Little Isaac was the first of that vast number.

## 2. GOD ASKS ABRAHAM FOR A SACRIFICIAL GIFT
### Genesis 22:1-8

Years later a strange thing happened. Let's suppose that Isaac could tell us about it himself. This, I think, is what he would say:

"Early one morning my father came into my tent. He woke me, saying, 'Hurry! Get ready. God has commanded that I offer a burnt-offering sacrifice to Him in the land of Moriah. Come. The servants have saddled the donkey and the wood is prepared.'

"I got ready as quickly as I could and we started on the long trip. I always enjoyed going places with my father. This time, however, he was unusually quiet. Oh, he answered any questions that I asked. But he seemed to have something on his mind–something that troubled him."

### Show Illustration #2

"All day we traveled and that night we slept under the stars. The next day we went on and on. And again we slept under the stars. I loved looking at the stars. I tried to count them, for God had promised my parents that there would be more people in their family than stars in the sky. And I was the first of that number.

"On our third day of traveling, my father spotted the mountain in Moriah where he was to worship God. To his servants he said, 'You stay here with the donkey. Isaac and I will go and worship and come again to you.' My father gave the wood to me to carry. He carried the fire and a knife. We started up the hill, but something was missing. 'Father,' I said, 'here is the wood and the fire. But where is the lamb for the burnt offering?'

"'My son,' my father answered, 'God will provide Himself a lamb for a burnt offering.' So we quietly climbed together."

## 3. GOD TESTS ABRAHAM BY ASKING FOR HIS SON
### Genesis 22:9-19

"Finally we got to the place about which God had told my father. Gathering stones, my father built an altar and laid the wood upon it. Then, turning to me, my father bound me with ropes. And I realized that God had asked him to offer me, the son he loved. Me! I was to be killed. I, Isaac, was the sacrifice!

### Show Illustration #3

"My father laid me upon the wood on the altar and raised the knife over me. Tears ran down his face. He loved me; I knew it. As much as my father loved me, he loved God even more.

"But at that very moment the angel of the Lord called out of Heaven, saying, 'Abraham, Abraham! Do not lay your hand on Isaac. For now I know that you fear God, seeing you have not withheld your son, your only son, from Me.'

"My father turned and saw behind him a ram caught in the bush by his horns. And we knew then that God had provided a substitute animal sacrifice. Father untied me, took the ram and offered it as a burnt offering in place of me.

"Again the voice called, 'Because you have obeyed Me and have not held back your son, your only son, I will greatly bless you. In your family shall all the nations of the earth be blessed.'

"No one else can ever know how happy my father and I were as we returned to the servants and started the journey home together. God had tested my father, Abraham, with the hardest of all tests. Because my father trusted God (see Hebrews 11: 17-19), he willingly obeyed Him."

This, I think, is what Isaac would have told us if he were here.

## 4. ALL BELIEVERS CAN GIVE THEMSELVES TO GOD
### Romans 12:1-2

Today God is asking you to give *yourself* to Him. He waits for your obedience. Are you willing for Him to use you in whatever way He desires? I cannot know what God wants you to do. But each member of God's family receives gifts from God that enable him to serve God in some way. (See Romans 12:6-8; 1 Corinthians 12:1-11; Ephesians 4:7-12.)

### Show Illustration #4A

Some Christians are given the gift of preaching. So they should preach.

### Show Illustration #4B

Others are given the gift of teaching. They should teach. Some have the gift of speaking words that comfort and help others. They should speak such words. Almost all Christians have some earthly treasure which they can share with others. This they should do in a simple way, not drawing attention to themselves. Those who have the gift of leading others should lead them. Perhaps the Lord is asking you to serve Him in one way or more.

In daily life there are many things we can do as "living sacrifices." We should genuinely love others. We should hate sin. We should show respect for each other. We should not be lazy. We should always work hard.

### Show Illustration #4C

We should not let anything stop us from praying. We should pray for those who make trouble for us. We should share our home and what we have with those in need. We should be happy with those who are happy. We should be sad with those who are sad. We should live peacefully with each other. We should not be proud of ourselves or of what we do. If someone who hates us is hungry, we should feed him. If he is thirsty, we should give him something to drink. We should not let sin have power over us. We should let good have power over sin.

These things and others are listed for us in Romans 12, immediately following the command of God to present our bodies to Him as living sacrifices. By practicing them, we shall be living sacrifices–living lives that please God. Will you offer yourself to God right now? Will each of you tell something which you believe God wants you to do this week as an obedient living sacrifice? (After sharing these things, have silent prayer so each one may promise God what he will do, with His help.)

In our notebooks under the title: CHRISTIAN SACRIFICE (Romans 12) let us list the things we can do as living sacrifices for God (verses 6-21).

# Lesson 2
# CHRISTIAN OBEDIENCE

**Scripture to be studied:** Romans 13:1-7; Matthew 17:24-27; Mark 12:13-17; Daniel 3:1-30

**The *aim* of the lesson:** To teach that Christians must be good examples of obedience and allegiance to both God and country.

**What your students should *know*:** Christians are to obey the rulers of the land, but they must first be obedient to God.

**What your students should *feel*:** A desire to obey God and do His will.

**What your students should *do*:** Determine what they will do for God as His living sacrifices.

**Lesson outline (for the teacher's and students' notebooks):**
1. Jesus sets a good example by paying the tax (Matthew 17:24-27).
2. Christians must obey God (Matthew 17:27; Mark 12:13-17).
3. God's children may suffer when they obey God (Daniel 3:1-23).
4. God is with those who obey Him (Daniel 3:24-30).

**The verse to be memorized:**

*So then every one of us shall give account of himself to God.* (Romans 14:12)

### NOTE TO THE TEACHER

God, the righteous One, commands that all members of His family give themselves to Him as living sacrifices. (See Romans 12:1-2.) Immediately after that command are two lists: (1) of definite ways we can serve God and (2) of things we are to do in our everyday Christian lives.

In Romans 13:1-7 members of God's family are told the importance of obeying government authorities. Today there is much rebellion against authority–rebellion against government, against teachers, against parents. Young people and adults need to understand the clear teachings of the Word of God.

## REVIEW

1. To whom will each of us have to give account of himself? (*To God*)
2. What kind of sacrifices are Christians to be? (*Living sacrifices*)
3. Name some ways in which "living sacrifices" can serve God. (*Preaching; teaching; speaking comforting, helpful words; sharing what they have with others without drawing attention to themselves; leading.*)
4. Name some things which a "living sacrifice" Christian can do in his everyday life. (*Love others genuinely; hate sin; show respect for others; he/she should not be lazy; work hard; pray; share his/her home and posessions with those in need; pray for those who make trouble for him/her; be happy with those who are happy; be sad with those who are sad; live peacefully with others; not be proud of him/herself or of what he/she does; feed and give drink to those who hate him/her; not let sin have power over him/her; let good have power over sin.*)
5. Because Abraham trusted God, what did he do? (*He obeyed God by being willing to offer his son, Isaac.*)
6. Who will tell us the lesson about Abraham offering Isaac? (*Teacher:* Let the student who responds use the illustrations in this book.)
7. Last week some of you offered yourselves to God as living sacrifices. Were you a living sacrifice this past week? Will you tell us now something you did for Him?

## THE LESSON

Juan (*Teacher:* Use any name familiar to your group) had a problem. His teacher had explained that since he had received Christ as his Saviour, he was a citizen of Heaven–a member of the family of God. His loyalty now belonged to God and His heavenly kingdom, rather than to this earth. His teacher had said, "We're still in the world, but we shouldn't be part of the world. As living sacrifices to God, we should be separated from the things of the world."

Juan was puzzled. He understood that he now had a new life in Christ. He understood that he belonged to God's family. But did that mean that he shouldn't be obedient to the laws of his land? Should he pay tax money to the government, even though that money might be used in wrong ways? How could Juan find the answers to these questions?

Long ago, in the Apostle Paul's day, the Roman believers must have been asking the same questions Juan asked. So Paul speaks about these matters in his letter to the Romans (chapter 13): "Every one of you should be obedient to those in power. There is no power on earth except that which is allowed by God. If a person doesn't obey the leaders of the land, he's working against God." Please write in your notebook:

### Christian Obedience
**Romans 13:1-7**

"Obey the laws of the land."

"Pay your taxes."

"Give respect to those in authority."

(*Teacher*: Have students list the above in their notebooks.)

## 1. JESUS SETS A GOOD EXAMPLE BY PAYING THE TAX
**Matthew 17:24-27**

Even before Paul wrote his letter, the Lord Jesus Christ had explained the importance of obeying the laws of the land. And, by His example, He showed all Christians what they should do.

### Show Illustration #5

On one occasion, some men approached Peter and asked, "Does your Master pay tax money for the temple of

– 20 –

God?" Every person was required to pay this tax to be used for the expenses of the house of God.

Peter answered, "Yes, my Master pays the tax money."

Later, the Lord Jesus asked him, "Peter, from whom do the kings of this earth get their tax money? Do they get it from their own children or from others outside their family?"

Peter answered, "From those outside their families."

"That is right," Jesus said. "Their children are free from having to pay the tax money."

Jesus was saying that because He is the Son of God, He would not really be required to pay the tax money for the worship of God. Peter understood that Jesus is the Son of God. But the tax collectors and other people didn't understand that. So they would feel that Jesus disobeyed the law if He refused to pay His money. Therefore Jesus said, "We won't do anything to offend these people. We will set a good example by paying the tax."

## 2. CHRISTIANS MUST OBEY GOD
### Matthew 17:27; Mark 12:13-17

### Show Illustration #6A

Then Jesus gave a strange command to Peter. "Go down to the sea and cast in a hook," He said. "Look in the mouth of the first fish that you catch. In it you will find a piece of money. Take it and pay My taxes and yours."

Jesus, the Son of God, set an example of obedience to all who would be His followers. He proved He was a good citizen by obeying the laws of the land.

Again, two groups of men (Pharisees, the religious law-keepers and Herodians, Herod's men) asked Jesus a question: "Teacher, we know that You are true. You are not afraid of what people think about You. You teach the way of God in truth. Now tell us, is it right for us to pay taxes to Caesar? Or should we not pay taxes?" Caesar was the Roman ruler, and many of the Jewish people thought that they should not be required to pay taxes to the Romans. If Jesus had said, "Yes, you should pay taxes," the Jews would have been angry. But if He had said, "No, you should not pay taxes," the Romans would have been angry. What should He do?

Because Jesus knew their wickedness, He understood that they were trying to trick Him. "Why do you try to trap Me?" he asked. "Bring me a coin."

### Show Illustration #6B

When they brought the coin, Jesus said "Whose picture is on this coin? Whose name is on it?"

"It is Caesar's picture and name," the men answered.

"Then pay to Caesar the things which belong to Caesar. And pay to God the things that belong to God," Jesus told them.

The men could find no fault with Jesus' answer. They were amazed at His wisdom.

The Apostle Paul used almost these same words when he wrote to the Romans. He said, "Pay taxes to whom taxes are to be paid." This is the Word of God. God will give you wisdom to know His will and courage to obey it.

But suppose someone should try to force you to do something which is *against* God or His Word? What should the Christian do then? God's Word says we must obey God instead of men. (See Acts 5:29.) This means that if we have to make a choice, we are to obey God first, rather than men.

The apostle was told by the rulers of the land to stop preaching about the Lord Jesus Christ. But he knew that God had called him to preach. His first duty was to obey God. So he had to continue his preaching even if it meant going to prison.

## 3. GOD'S CHILDREN MAY SUFFER WHEN THEY OBEY GOD
### Daniel 3:1-23

Long before Paul lived, Daniel was ordered to stop praying to God. But because Daniel was a child of God, he knew he had to continue to pray. When he was thrown into the den of lions because he prayed, God protected him and spared his life.

Daniel had three friends who also loved God. Like Daniel, they were taken as captives to the land of Babylon. Nebuchadnezzar, the king of Babylon, was a proud and wicked man who commanded his people to make a large idol of gold. When the idol was finished, the king announced a great meeting.

The king's messenger cried out, "To you it is commanded, O people, that when you hear the sound of the musical instruments, you must fall down and worship the golden image that King Nebuchadnezzar has set up. Whoever does not fall down and worship shall be thrown into a burning, fiery furnace."

What should the three young men do? They did not want to disobey a law of the king. But they served the living God of Heaven. And God had said, "You shall have no other gods before Me. . . . You shall not bow down to them nor serve them." (See Exodus 20:2-5.) There was no question in their minds. The king had asked them to do something they could not do. They had to obey God rather than the king.

### Show Illustration #7

When the music sounded, the three refused to bow before the idol.

Someone told the king, "These men, O king, have not obeyed you. They do not serve your gods, nor do they worship the golden image which you have set up."

That made the king furious. He sent for the men and asked them, "Is it true that you do not serve my gods, nor worship the golden image which I have set up? If you do not worship the image, you will be cast the same hour into the midst of a burning, fiery furnace. And who is that God who will deliver you out of my hands?"

The men replied, "If God wills, He is able to save us from the burning fiery furnace, and He will deliver us out of your hand, O king. But if not, we will not serve your gods, nor worship the golden image which you have set up."

The king was filled with fury. He commanded, "Heat the furnace seven times hotter than it is usually heated." He ordered the mightiest men of his army, "Bind these men and cast them into the burning fiery furnace." The fire was so hot that it burned to death the men who threw the three into it.

## 4. GOD IS WITH THOSE WHO OBEY HIM
### Daniel 3:24-30

When the king looked into the furnace, he was astonished. He said to his men, "Did we cast three men bound into the fire?" They answered, "True, O king."

### Show Illustration #8

The king said, "But I see four men loose, walking in the fire. They are not hurt. And the form of the fourth is like the Son of God."

Then the king called to the three, "You servants of the Most High God, come out and come here."

The king and his men saw the three, upon whose bodies the fire had had no effect. Not a hair of their heads was scorched. Their clothing didn't even smell of smoke. Three young men had chosen to obey God, and God Himself had been with them, to protect them.

God expects us to be obedient to the rulers of our land. But above all, He wants us to obey Him and put His will first. Will you obey God? Will you purpose to do His will? How will you do His will in the week ahead?

(*Teacher:* Have students discuss this, please.)

## Lesson 3
# CHRISTIAN LOVE

> **NOTE TO THE TEACHER**
>
> The narratives in the Bible are usually quite condensed. But because the people and the events are much like those of today, we believe more took place than is recorded. You will have to use your imagination to fill in some of the details. Occasionally you may wish to explain that we do not know exactly all that happened. But from what we're told, it must have happened this way–the way we tell it.
>
> If you will always remember, teacher, that the people who lived during Bible times were much like we are, it will help you to make the people live to your students. Put yourself in the place of the man who was robbed and beaten and left half dead. How would you feel? Or if you were the Samaritan who saw an enemy Jew lying in the road, what would be your reaction? Think this through carefully before telling this account and all others.
>
> Use dialogue whenever you can. Your characters will live if they do the talking. Instead of simply saying that the man was wounded and beaten, have him cry to the passerby, "Wait! Help! Don't leave me here to die."
>
> Your voice should express the feeling of the narrative. Imitation of the characters will make the lesson real.
>
> Practice to develop a quality of voice that is pleasant.
>
> Keep your eyes on your students. Your eyes should contact theirs throughout the entire lesson.
>
> Be enthusiastic in your teaching. There is nothing that equals enthusiasm. Study well so that the truths of the lesson are a part of you. Then you can speak from experience and that will make you enthusiastic.

**Scripture to be studied:** Romans 13:8-14; Luke 10:25-37

**The *aim* of the lesson:** To help your students understand God's law of love.

**What your students should *know*:** When Christians give themselves to God, God's love fills their heart so they can love others.

**What your students should *feel*:** A desire to love others.

**What your students should *do*:** Ask God for the power to love others more than themselves.

**Lesson outline (for the teacher's and students' notebooks):**

1. Jesus tells of a pitiful man who needs love (Luke 10:25-30).
2. Two men show no love for the unfortunate man (Luke 10:31-32).
3. A Samaritan proves his love by his deed (Luke 10:33-37).

**The verse to be memorized:**

*So then every one of us shall give account of himself to God.* (Romans 14:12)

## REVIEW

1. We have learned that all believers in the Lord Jesus Christ are to present themselves to God as a living sacrifice to be used in any way God wants. For some this will mean that they will always serve only God. According to Romans 12, what kind of service might this be? (*Preaching. Teaching. Speaking comforting, helpful words. Sharing what they have with others without drawing attention to themselves. Leading others.*)
2. All of us–for we are all servants of God–are required to do certain things in our everyday lives because we are living sacrifices. What things are these, according to Romans 12? (*We are to love others genuinely. We are to hate sin. We are to show respect for others. We should not be lazy. We should work hard. We should pray. We should share our homes and whatever we have with those in need. We should pray for those who make trouble for us. We should be happy with those who are happy. We should be sad with those who are sad. We should live peacefully with others. We should not be proud of ourselves or of what we do. We should give food and drink to the hungry and thirsty. We should not let sin have power over us. We should let good have power over sin.*)
3. Our memory verse tells us that we must all give account of ourselves to whom? (*God*)
4. We have learned also that Christians are to obey the laws of the land. According to Romans 13:1-7, whom are we to obey? (*The leaders of the land*)
5. Who gives the leaders of the land their power? (*God*)
6. Who allows certain ones to be leaders? (*God*)
7. If a person does not obey the leaders of the land, against whom is he/she working? (*God*)
8. Are Christians to pay taxes? (*Yes*)
9. The Lord Jesus was not required to pay temple taxes because He is the Son of God and all worship belongs to Him. Did He pay the temple tax? (*Yes*)
10. If one must choose between obeying God and obeying the laws of the land, which is he to choose? (*Obeying God*)
11. If God has called us to preach or to teach but the leaders

of the land say we are not allowed to preach or teach, whom must we obey? (*God*)

### Show Illustration #9A

12. What happened to Paul when he obeyed God by preaching? (*He was put in jail.*)
13. If God wants us to pray but the leaders say we are not allowed to pray, whom should we obey? (*God*)

### Show Illustration #9B

14. What happened to Daniel when he obeyed God by praying? (*He was cast into the lions' den.*)
15. If the laws of the land say we are to worship and serve idols rather than God, what are Christians to do? (*Serve God only. Christians should* not *worship or serve idols.*)
16. What happened to the three Hebrews who refused to worship the golden image which Nebuchadnezzar had set up? (*They were cast into the burning fiery furnace.*)

### Show Illustration #8

17. Did God forsake them there? (*No, the Son of God was with them to protect them in the furnace.*)
18. Did you obey God rather than men this past week? In what way?

### THE LESSON

Paul reminded the Roman believers, and also reminds us that we are to give ourselves to God as living sacrifices. He also taught that Christians are to be obedient to the laws of the land. Then he explained that Christians have another responsibility–they are to love others. Some of the Romans apparently thought that the only thing they had to do was to obey the commandments of God. Of course it's expected that Christians will obey His laws: they will not murder; they will not steal; they will not lie. God expects obedience in these matters and many others. But obeying such commandments isn't all that God expects. Paul said that you will only fulfill God's law if you truly love others. Will you write in your notebooks, please:

**Christian Love**
Romans 13:8-10

## 1. JESUS TELLS OF A PITIFUL MAN WHO NEEDS LOVE
### Luke 10:25-30

One day a group of men asked the Lord Jesus about these very things. One of them who knew God's law asked, "Teacher, what shall I do to inherit eternal life?"

The Lord Jesus answered, "What is written in the law? What does the law say?"

The man replied, "You must love the Lord your God with all your heart. You must love Him with all your soul. You must love Him with all your mind. You must love Him with all your strength. You must love your neighbor as you love yourself." Trying to make himself look good, he asked, "Who is my neighbor?"

### Show Illustration #10

To answer his question, the Lord Jesus told him this story: "One day, a certain man–a Jew–began a journey from Jerusalem to Jericho. As he traveled, a group of thieves grabbed him, took his clothes, beat him and left him by the side of the road, half dead.

## 2. TWO MEN SHOW NO LOVE FOR THE UNFORTUNATE MAN
### Luke 10:31-32

"Later the man heard footsteps. He turned to see who was coming. It was a priest–a servant of God. The man was certain that help had come. But the footsteps did not slow down. The priest seemed to walk faster. The wounded man turned to see the priest cross the road and hurry by on the other side. 'Wait! Help!' he cried weakly. 'Don't leave me here to die!' But the priest rushed on, never looking back. Why had the priest passed by and left him to die? How could he be so cruel?

"The man thought: *If I should die, who will take care of my wife and children?* Worry mixed with pain as he lay there, helpless and bleeding.

"But listen! Footsteps again."

### Show Illustration #11

"Yes! Someone was coming. It was a man of the family group of Levi.

"Oh, this time he would be helped! The Levite paused, looked at the wounded man, then crossed to the other side of the road and kept going.

## 3. A SAMARITAN PROVES HIS LOVE BY HIS DEED
### Luke 10:33-37

"Footsteps again. But it was only a Samaritan. He would surely pass by, for the Samaritans and the Jews were enemies of each other The injured man thought, *If men from my own country won't help me, neither will a Samaritan*.

### Show Illustration #12

"But the Samaritan knelt beside the bleeding man. Tenderly he cleaned the wounds with oil and wine and bandaged him. Then the Samaritan lifted him onto his donkey, supporting him so he wouldn't fall.

"Slowly they went to an inn. 'We'll rest here,' the Samaritan explained. All night long he stayed by the wounded man's side, caring for him, giving him sips of cool water and bathing his wounds. The next morning the Samaritan had to leave. Taking some of his own money, he gave it to the keeper of the inn, saying, 'I'll pay you to take care of this man. It if costs more than I've given you, I'll repay you when I pass this way again.'"

Jesus had finished His story. His listeners were silent. "Now," said Jesus, "which of these three men was a neighbor to the one who fell among the thieves?" Finally one man answered, "He who showed mercy on him." Jesus responded by saying, "You go and do likewise."

Do you suppose that the priest and the Levite truly loved God with all their heart, soul, mind and strength? Did they love others as much as they loved themselves? Or did they love themselves most of all?

Paul wanted the Roman believers–and us–to understand God's law of love. He gave some very plain suggestions for showing love toward others. Listen carefully to his words. Then write them in your notebook under the title, *Christian Love*.

How many of these things are you practicing in your own life?

1. Do not owe anyone anything–except love.
2. Obey God by loving your neighbor.
   a. Do not kill anyone.
   b. Do not steal.
   c. Do not lie.
   d. Do not want something for yourself that belongs to someone else.

These commands and the others are all part of this commandment: "You must love your neighbor as yourself."

If you love your neighbor you won't do any wrong to him/her.

3. Do not get drunk.
4. Do not quarrel or be jealous.
5. Let every part of you–from head to foot–belong to the Lord Jesus Christ.
6. Do not let your wicked thoughts lead you to do sinful things.

I'm certain that you wish that people around you were like this. Well, this is the kind of Christian they would like *you* to be! What's more, this is the way *God* wants you to live. Of course these things are hard to do, even impossible, if we try to live up to them in our own strength. But God sees our thoughts. He knows our attitudes. He knows if we are willing to live His way. If we are willing, He'll give us the power to do these things.

Together, let's read the list aloud from our notebooks.

Do you want to be given over to God completely to be a living sacrifice for His glory? Do you want to be so filled with His love that you can love others as much as you love yourself? One day each one of us will give an account to God. If your trust is in the Lord Jesus Christ, will you decide now to live the life of Christian love? Ask God for the power to do it. (*Teacher*: give opportunity for silent prayer.)

# Lesson 4
# THE CHRISTIAN LIFE

**Scripture to be studied:** Romans 14; Luke 6:1-11

**The *aim* of the lesson:** To emphasize that God, who is righteous in all His acts, desires to live through the lives of His own.

**What your students should *know*:** God wants each Christian to live righteously.

**What your students should *feel*:** A desire to let God live His life through them.

**What your students should *do*:** Live today in such a way that they will not be ashamed when they stand before Christ.

**Lesson outline (for the teacher's and students' notebooks):**

1. We are not to judge others (Romans 14:1-4).
2. We must determine how God wants us to live (Luke 6:1-11; Romans 14:5-9).
3. We must prepare to face God's judgment (Romans 14:10-12).
4. We are not to offend others (Romans 14:13-23).

**NOTE TO THE TEACHER**

This is the last lesson on the book of Romans. It would be good to check your students' notebooks to see that they have a complete outline of the book with Scripture references.

If at all possible, take the time to review the entire book by using all the review questions in all five volumes (Condemnation; Justification; Sanctification; God and Israel; Living the Christian Life). Encourage your students to share with their classmates exactly how they have shown Christian love during the past week.

Emphasize again that the theme of the book is *The Righteousness of God*. God is righteous in all His acts. And His desire is that His righteousness will be lived through the lives of those who trust in Him. Please stress that truth.

**The verse to be memorized:**

*So then every one of us shall give account of himself to God.* (Romans 14:12)

## THE LESSON

Let's do a bit of make-believe today. Suppose that you are going to take a long journey–away from the town in which you live, away from your country, away across the ocean, to live in a foreign land. At first, all would seem very different. The people would probably look different to you. They might have different colored skin and hair. They might dress differently. They would speak another language. Their customs would not be like yours. The food might seem strange to you and you would have to learn to eat it. If you were to go to live in a new land, you would have to learn many new ways and adjust your life accordingly.

In some ways, this is what happens when a person becomes a believer in the Lord Jesus Christ. Believers are members of a new family–God's family. Believers are citizens of a new country–Heaven. At first we may wonder how a Christian should act and how he should talk. We know that our lives will be different from what they were before we received the Lord Jesus as Saviour. We will understand God's Word in a new way. For some, it may mean worshiping in a new way. We will find our interests changing. Our desires will be different from what they once were.

In the Apostle Paul's day, there was some confusion concerning the Christian's life. What should he eat or not eat? How should he talk? What was right? What was wrong? Paul wished to settle these matters for the believers in Rome–and for us. So he gave four simple rules to follow. It will be helpful to us who are believers in Christ to remember these rules. Let's list them in our notebooks under the heading:

**The Christian Life**
**Romans 14**

## 1. WE ARE NOT TO JUDGE OTHERS
### Romans 14:1-4

### Show Illustration #13

Some believers in Paul's time argued about what foods they should eat. Some said that a Christian should not eat meat because their heathen neighbors offered meat to idols. Many times that same meat was then sold in the marketplace as food. They said, "Surely it would be wrong for a Christian to eat meat which has been offered to an idol as a sacrifice." Others said, "The meat itself has done no wrong. How can it possibly hurt me? My salvation depends on my faith in the Lord Jesus, not on the food I eat." And so they argued.

Paul wrote, "You should not judge each other." God is the only One who has the right to judge. The eating of meat, or not eating meat, is not the important matter. But the attitude of believers toward each other *is* important.

Are you guilty of the same sort of thing? Sometimes we may have our own ideas as to what a Christian should eat. If someone else has a different idea, are we quick to criticize him/her? Do we think that he/she is less spiritual than we are? Remember the verse we have been memorizing: "every one of us shall give account of *himself* to God."

## 2. WE MUST DETERMINE HOW GOD WANTS US TO LIVE
### Luke 6:1-11; Romans 14:5-9

Some of the Hebrew Christians continued to observe the Jewish Sabbath (Saturday) as their fathers and grandfathers had done before the death and resurrection of the Lord Jesus Christ. They felt that the laws which had been given to them hundreds of years before the coming of the Lord Jesus should still be observed. Others felt that the first day of the week (Sunday) should be observed as a day of worship in honor of the resurrection of the Lord from the grave. Still others felt that the day itself held no special honor. For a Christian, every day should be set apart for service to the Lord.

There was also some disagreement as to what could be done on the day of worship.

### Show Illustration #14A

The Lord Jesus too had been faced with this problem. One day He and His disciples were walking through a grain field on the Sabbath day. The disciples, being hungry, picked some of the grain and began to eat. This was permitted any day–except the Sabbath. Some of the Jews saw it and criticized them.

### Show Illustration #14B

A little later, Jesus went to the synagogue and saw a man with a crippled hand. Again, the Jews tried to find fault with Jesus by saying, "Is it right or wrong to heal on the Sabbath day?"

Jesus answered them with a question. "If one of you has a sheep which falls into a pit on the Sabbath day, will you reach down and help it out of the pit? If so, then how much better is a man than a sheep?" Then, turning to the man with the crippled hand, Jesus healed him by His word.

Jesus was showing the people that the attitude of each person's heart is important. What we do, or what we don't do, should be for the glory of God. All that we do should be done as to the Lord. That is, we should live in a manner which pleases Him. Each one of us is responsible for knowing what we ourselves should do to please Him.

That is what it says here in Romans: "Every one must be sure in his own mind" what God wants him to do (Romans l4:5b). We must know what God wants us to do.

This doesn't mean that we are free to do anything we want to do. God's Word must be the guide, and the Holy Spirit of God must be our teacher. We must always obey God's Word.

## 3. WE MUST PREPARE TO FACE GOD'S JUDGMENT
### Romans 14:10-12

### Show Illustration #15

Here we are reminded that one day each believer will stand individually before the Lord to give account to Him for the way he or she has lived his/her Christian life. We will not be condemned to eternal punishment for our sins. Christ has died for our sins, and if we have placed our trust in Him, we have been pronounced righteous. But we will be *responsible* for the lives which we have lived–whether we have obeyed or disobeyed God's Word.

Sometimes we may wonder whether it is right or wrong to do a certain thing. What should we do? First, we ought to see whether God's Word has anything to say about it. The Bible says that certain things, such as stealing and lying, are definitely wrong. There can be no question about such sin. But other things may not be mentioned by name; so we are not sure what to do. We should always ask ourselves: "When I stand before the Lord, will I have to be ashamed that I have done this thing?" When we talk to God in prayer, we should ask Him to show us what we should or should not do.

## 4. WE ARE NOT TO OFFEND OTHERS
### Romans 14:13-23

Here we read that Christians should be good examples to others. Someone else may be watching the way you live and looking at the things you do. Be careful that you are not causing that person to do something wrong.

### Show Illustration #16

You wouldn't deliberately place a stone in someone's path, knowing it would cause that person to fall. So we learn in this part of the Word of God that it is not good to eat meat or to drink wine, or to do anything by which another might fall into sin. Does this mean that it is wrong to eat meat? Oh, no. Some of the Hebrew Christians would not eat meat because they were afraid it might have been used in the worship of idols. The meat itself was good to eat. Eating it would not dishonor God. But if someone would be harmed by seeing the Christian eat that meat, then the Christian should not eat it.

Why should we be so careful? Because we are to love others better than ourselves. We should be concerned about how they feel. We should not want anyone to be weakened because of us. Why did Paul say he would not drink wine? Sometimes wine was used as a medicine. Paul could have used it in this way without sinning. But suppose another Christian whose faith was weak should see Paul drinking wine. He might drink it also. But he might drink so much that he would become drunk. Paul did not want to be responsible for another man's drunkenness. So he tried to keep from doing anything that would cause another to sin.

These four rules, then, should help us Christians in our actions: we should not judge others; we must determine how God wants us to live; we must prepare to stand before the Lord and give account of our Christian lives; we are not to offend others, If our everyday living is guided by these rules, we can feel certain that God's righteousness will be ours.

Before we close the book of Romans, let's review once again what it is all about:

1. What is the theme of the book? (*The righteousness of God*)
2. Is God righteous in condemning sinners? (*Yes*)
3. How many have sinned? (*All*)
4. What is the meaning of condemnation? (*It means to declare guilty; to prove guilty; to sentence to punishment.*)
5. What is the meaning of justification? (*It means to declare righteous.*)
6. How may a person be declared righteous? (*By placing his/her trust in the Lord Jesus Christ*)
7. How can God, the righteous One, declare righteous those sinners who have received the Saviour? (*He does it by placing our sins on the Lord Jesus. At the same time He clothes the trusting sinner with Christ's righteousness.*)
8. What does sanctification mean? (*It means to be set apart by God for His purpose.*)
9. When are people sanctified? (*The moment they place their trust in the Lord Jesus Christ*)
10. Was God righteous in choosing Israel for His own? (*Yes*)
11. Has God been righteous in cutting off Israel? (*Yes*)
12. Why has God rejected Israel? (*Because Israel rejected Him*)
13. Is there a bright future for Israel? (*Yes. There is a day coming when many Israelites will receive the Lord Jesus as Saviour and King.*)
14. Does God ask all Christians to be living sacrifices? (*Yes*)
15. Who must give account of himself to God? (*Every person*)

www.ingramcontent.com/pod-product-compliance
Lightning Source LLC
Chambersburg PA
CBHW060804090426
42736CB00002B/157